Believing in
a Grand Thing

Also by Jim H. Ainsworth

Novels

Circle of Hurt

Rails to a River: A Long Awakening

Firstborn Son

Go Down Looking

Home Light Burning

Rivers Ebb

Rivers Crossing

In the Rivers Flow

Rivers Flow–2nd Edition

Business • Financial Planning • Financial Services

How to Become a Successful Financial Consultant

First Edition 1997 • Second Edition 2013

Recollections and True Stories

A River of Stories…It's Been Quite a Ride

Biscuits Across the Brazos

Believing in a Grand Thing

STORIES OF FAITH

Jim H. Ainsworth

First Edition

ISBN 978-0-9904628-3-5

Most of this work previously published as part of
A *River of Stories* by Jim H. Ainsworth.

Design by Vivian Freeman, *Yellow Rose Typesetting*

Printed in the United States of America

Season of Harvest Publications
2403 CR 4208
Campbell, Texas 75422

For the Unprepared, Old Age may be the Winter of Life.
For the Prepared, it's the Season of Harvest.

Front Cover Photo
Marion Ainsworth pays homage at his father's grave
in Shiloh Cemetery at the end of a 325-mile horseback journey.

In memory of my double cousin and great friend . . .

MARION SHEPHERD AINSWORTH.

*Through thick and thin, good and bad—
we laughed . . . we cried . . . we rode the trails . . .
we crossed the rivers . . . together.*

You are missed.

Believing in a Grand Thing

Even if there be no hereafter, I would live my time
believing in a grand thing that ought to be true if it is not...
I will go farther, and say I would rather die forever more
believing as Jesus believed, then live forever more
believing as those who deny him.

—From Frederick Buechner's
memoir, *Telling Secrets*

Contents

Life is lived forward,
but understood backward.
—Sören Kierkegaard

Introduction

A River of Stories... It's Been Quite a Ride, a collection of true stories, drew more personal responses from readers than any book I have written with the possible exception of my first novel, *In the Rivers Flow.* Most wrote about the final section, *Believing in a Grand Thing.* Their words are very rewarding and inspirational. Some readers battled life-threatening diseases; some struggled with life-changing events; some just appreciated an affirmation of their faith and to know they are not alone on life's journey.

In this section, I tell stories of my long, meandering and often interrupted journey toward faith from the viewpoint of a layman not well-versed in theology. But I supplement my personal experiences with wisdom from those I consider to be among the best Christian apologists, pastors, theologians, and writers. I share my doubts as well as epiphanies on life's journey.

Many expressed a desire to have this last section printed in a small book. Here it is, complete with a few extra words at the end to honor a lost loved one.

Thanks for sticking with me.

Jim

Believing in a Grand Thing

Stories of Faith

All I have seen teaches me to trust
the Creator for all I have not seen.
                        —Ralph Waldo Emerson

When the Student
Is Ready,
the Master Will Appear

Ever had a child, spouse, client or friend talk about a book read, a seminar attended, a lecture heard, that revealed some great secret or answer to a question they have been pondering for a lifetime? Ever listen to their enthusiasm, all the while wanting to shout that you have been trying to tell them this secret for years? Don't blame them. The author, speaker, or teacher they heard spoke to them. You may not have. It could have been because they knew you too well or just that the message had to be delivered by a stranger. In my old business, we often referred to an expert as a person with a briefcase who has traveled more than a hundred miles. There's a lot of truth to that. We listen to these experts while we fail to hear the same wisdom from familiar sources. Even Jesus said, *"Truly I tell you, no prophet is accepted in his hometown."*

We all know the old proverb, *"When the student (pupil) is ready, the master (teacher) will appear."* I dabbled around the fringes of C. S. Lewis's writings for many years. I quoted him in many seminars and training sessions, even though I had read only excerpts from his work (I plead guilty). I decided it was about time for "the teacher to appear."

Clyde Staples Lewis preferred to be called Jack. If you are not familiar with him, I suggest starting with the movie *Shadowlands*. Anthony Hopkins plays Lewis in this excellent rendition of a part of Lewis's life. I collect quotations about writing and reading and use them to defend my writing habit during times when there seems to be no rational justification for it. This movie provided one of the best. "*We read to know that we are not alone.*" We also write to find out if we are alone. What does that mean to you?

To me, it means we read to vicariously experience situations such as illness, death, murder, betrayal, great business success or failure, and athletic or artistic accomplishment. We need to see how characters in books react to situations we may have experienced, want to experience or just wondered about. We see also that other people in other places might have troubles worse than our own. We see places where they live, places we will likely never visit. This provides regular reassurance that "we are not alone."

C. S. Lewis is probably best known for his *Chronicles of Narnia* series (*The Lion, the Witch and the Wardrobe*, etc.). He was also close friends with J. R. R. Tolkien of *Lord of the Rings* fame. Both were on the English faculty at Oxford. But the book I am writing about is *Mere Christianity*. I perused it many years ago, but didn't apply myself. I picked it up about a year ago and read it again, this time with a highlighter and post-it notes. I wondered, for heaven's sake (a cliché meant to be taken literally here), why I had not done so before. After all, a boy's struggle to understand was partially revealed in this early passage from *Rivers Flow.*

> *After nine weeks of perfect attendance at Sunday school and church in Klondike, Jake heard the teacher ask the question he had been dreading. "Please raise your hands if you have been saved by accepting Jesus Christ as your personal savior." All of his classmates raised their hands. Jake sat on his.*

And there is this later passage where Jake is in church again.

> *As the sun rose higher, one of the spiraling dust tunnels focused on Jake, and he felt himself floating above the congregation, his mind drifting back to events that seemed so long ago.*

Several things sparked my revived lifelong need to understand (most would not interest you). I have written previously about the Cowhill Council, a group of seasoned sages who meet regularly for coffee. I make no pretense that our discussions are usually highly intellectual, but occasionally we try. One morning, we were fortunate enough to have two evangelists and a fellow in the middle of the rigorous training required to become a Catholic Deacon present for our meeting. I stuck my neck out and asked if anyone could explain the Crucifixion, Resurrection and Atonement in terms that an ignorant mortal like me could understand and spiritually absorb.

Everyone stared at me as if I had just arrived on planet Earth and never set foot in a church. But then, their faces lit up as they launched into vigorous attempts to comply. It led to a vibrant and enjoyable discussion, but their explanations were the same ones I had heard all my life. I was reminded of what Pastor Rick Warren said about the Holy Trinity, "*To deny the Holy Trinity is to lose your soul. To explain it is to lose your mind. God is God, I am not.*"

C. S. Lewis speaks to me. He lost his mother at nine. Raised in the Church of Ireland, he turned atheist at fifteen, even became interested in the occult, quoting Lucretius, "*Had God designed the world it would not be, a world so frail and faulty as we see.*" But he slowly re-embraced Christianity, influenced by his friend Tolkien and by his own "teacher" G. K. Chesterton and his book, *The Everlasting Man*.

In *Mere Christianity*, Lewis explains the Atonement and Resurrection this way:

> *The only person who could do it perfectly (repentance) would be the perfect person—and He would not need it. But supposing God became a man—suppose our human nature which can suffer and die was amalgamated with God's nature in one person—then that person could help us. He could surrender His will, and suffer and die, because He was man; and He could do it perfectly because He was God.*
>
> *You and I can go through this process only if God does it in us; but God can do it only if He becomes man. Our attempts at this dying will succeed only if we men share in God's dying, just as our thinking can succeed only because it is a drop out of the ocean of His intelligence. But we cannot share God's dying unless God dies, and He cannot die except by being a man. That is the sense in which He pays our debt and suffers for us what* HE NEED NOT SUFFER AT ALL.

Read that last sentence aloud. That explanation makes sense out of deep complexity.

And as for my wondering about God's punishment, Lewis has these words:

> A Christian is not a man who never goes wrong, but
> a man who is enabled to repent and pick himself up
> and begin over again after each stumble—because
> the Christ-life is inside him, repairing him all the time,
> enabling him to repeat (in some degree) the kind of
> voluntary death Christ Himself carried out...the
> Christian thinks any good he does comes from the
> Christ-life inside him. He does not think God will love
> us because we are good, but that God will make us
> good because He loves us.

There are many, many more explanations, of course. But that one does it for me. God recognized our weakness and knew we would continue to sin in spite of being shown miracle after miracle, with the most miraculous being the Resurrection and Ascension. So does that mean we mortals can just keep right on sinning because Jesus provided a permanent pathway to forgiveness? Yes and no. Yes, because we have been given a path to forgiveness. No, because purposeful, careless sinning means we don't really believe. If we have faith, we will exert every effort to live our lives following the example Jesus left for us. Yes, we will continue to be buffeted by doubts and be confronted with evil; we will continue to sin because we are weak, but we will recognize evil, recognize our sins, confess them, and ask for forgiveness with love. Sincere prayer will protect us. We must recognize our sins by studying God's Word and ask for forgiveness in **faith.** We must believe.

*We have little to lose by believing,
and everything to lose if we don't.*
                              —Dinesh D'Souza

Is There Evidence
of Life After Death?

D inesh D'Souza explores this question in his book, *Life After Death: The Evidence*. I admit a certain attraction to the word *evidence* in the title. I knew the author first as a secular think tank intellectual. I have seen him debate the now deceased atheist (but brilliant) Christopher Hitchens, who acknowledged D'Souza as a world-class advocate for the Christian faith.

Rick Warren, author of *The Purpose Driven Life*, wrote the introduction to this book. *Death:*

> *The mortality rate on earth is 100 percent. This book
> by my friend Dinesh D'Souza is a brilliant investigation
> of the fascinating and crucial issue of what happens
> when we die. It is an inquiry based on scholarship and
> reason and it provides a convincing answer that is
> explosive in its impact.*

D'Souza deftly turns the table on scientists who say, "If they really believe in a life after death, why not conduct sound experiments to establish it?" D'Souza answers that religious believers don't believe in the afterlife based on scientific tests. He then challenges them to come up with some tests to prove or disprove it. Without such tests and empirical evidence, how can true scientists reject it? Atheists say that the absence of evidence is evidence of absence. D'Souza answers by saying *not found* is not the same thing as found not to exist.

Life After Death also explores near-death experiences including the out-of-body phenomenon, the tunnel of darkness, the bright light, the sensation of love and warmth, the life review, and subsequent life transformations. Evolution? Yep, D'Souza covers it, saying,

> . . . *contrary to atheist boasting, evolution cannot provide*
> *an ultimate explanation for life because evolution itself*
> *presupposes specific environmental conditions and*
> *specific entities with specific properties. The human*
> *cell, thousands of times tinier than a speck of dust,*
> *has the processing power equivalent to the largest*
> *supercomputer. So how did we get cells? How do they*
> *self-replicate? Darwin does not attempt to answer.*

In a later book, D'Souza explores another question he poses in debates with atheists: Why did it take mankind more than 85,000 years to figure out he could effectively communicate, make useful tools, and settle in one place to grow crops? Humans accomplished virtually nothing for ninety-eight percent of our existence, then abruptly in the last two percent, produced everything from the pyramids to Proust, Newton to nanotechnology.

D'Souza also says that evolution does a good job of accounting for why we are selfish animals, but it faces immense challenges in accounting for why we simultaneously hold that we *ought not to be selfish*.

In a chapter called "Good for You," D'Souza refers to William James, the founder of modern psychology. James makes the point that while belief in life after death poses the risk of adopting a position without complete proof...unbelief poses the risk of missing out on the blessings of immortality that are promised to believers. Makes sense to me. Who was it who said irreverently but also logically, "Why take a chance?"

Believers are provided with hope at death and a way to cope. For atheists, death is a disaster. Belief infuses life with an enhanced sense of meaning and purpose. Belief gives us a reason to be moral and a way to transfer that morality to our children. Finally, there is strong evidence that belief in life after death makes your life better and also makes you a better person.

On page 166, I found my favorite words from D'Souza.

> *Here is my pre-suppositional argument for life after death. Unlike material objects and all other living creatures, we humans inhabit two domains: the way things are, and the way things ought to be.*

Why is it my favorite passage? Because on page three of *Rivers' Flow*, Griffin Rivers says, *"Flow is the difference between the way things are and the way they ought to be."* I promise not to sue D'Souza for plagiarism. I'm kidding. Just a little more proof that similar threads run through all our stories, binding us together.

If not for evil and suffering, how would we appreciate painlessness and good?
—Gottfried Leibniz

Why Does God Let Bad Things Happen?

I hear this question stated more often as a statement by non-believers and others trying to come to grips with their faith. "How does one believe in a God that would let these kinds of things happen?" Remember Lucretius's quote that C. S. Lewis used when he was an atheist? *Had God designed the world it would not be, a world so frail and faulty as we see.* The quote does raise some doubts. If God is perfect, then why did he not design a perfect world? Why do bad things still happen?

Another book by Dinesh D'Souza, *God Forsaken: Bad Things Happen. Is there a God Who Cares? Yes: Here's Proof* addresses this question with boldness. Lucretius challenges our belief in a God who could have made a perfect world, but chose not to. D'Souza says the Divine Architect could not have made a perfect universe and have us human beings in it.

God intended us to be here to marvel at his architecture and get to know the Architect and enter into an intimate relationship of mutual love with Him.... He built the universe in the only way He could to get this result.

Christians praise God when good things happen to them, so should they also blame God when bad things happen to them? The book of Job has been recognized as one of the deepest, most candid examinations of the problem of evil and suffering. Yet remarkably, it never occurs to Job or to anyone else in the story to question God's existence. What Job questions is the character of God.

D'Souza says that omnipotence does not mean the power to do anything, but rather the power to do *what is possible.* And there is only one possible way to create a universe containing rational, conscious creatures like us—creatures who are prone to sin, evil and corruption. If the world was perfect, we wouldn't be allowed in it.

Do we suffer punishment here on earth for evil deeds? Do we get what we deserve? I explored this through Jake's character in *Rivers Flow* in this scene with Claire Hurt when Claire tells him,

> *Oh, I shook my fist at God, raging at His injustice*
> *to us. We were in church every Sunday morning and*
> *Sunday night, yet we lost our only child.*

Most of us, believers and non-believers who have lived long enough, know there is almost no direct correlation between pain and hardship and our virtues and vices. Earthquakes and tsunamis make no distinction between the just and unjust.

Rabbi Harold Kushner says in his book, *When Bad Things Happen to Good People,* "*It's simply a fact.*" Kushner also says that *God doesn't stop the bad things because He can't. So he does what he can to reduce evil and suffering, and He identifies with the victims.* But Dr. Charles Stanley says Scripture tells us that God has absolute authority over the world and lets evil enter the world because He desired love from the human beings He created. Love must be given freely, so God had to offer humans a choice. The only other choices were to not create or to create robotic-like humans without choice. The views of these religious scholars seem to conflict, but Kushner might be saying that God can't stop evil...because He allowed choice.

More confusion. Does this mean prayer can't work because God can't stop bad things from happening? No. The two words to remember are faith and love. If we pray with faith and love, we have made choices and then God can interfere, because these are the two things He wants from us. In *Rivers Flow*, Claire lets Jake explore his own anger at God, his feelings that he and his family did something to cause their loss. She answers him thusly:

> *We have a right to be hurt, even angry. Life is unfair, and God is there to help us when unfair things happen to us, not to prevent them from happening.*

Kushner says that God is as outraged by it as we are.

In the *Shadowlands* movie, Anthony Hopkins as Jack Lewis lectures to various audiences about the good that comes from suffering. In his book, *Theodicity*, Gottfried Leibniz says if not for evil and suffering, how would we appreciate painlessness and good? We need the one to appreciate the other, just as we need the night to appreciate sunrise.

Why does God let us sin? D'Souza says God sought to create a creature (us) that could reciprocate his love. Now, it is in the nature of love to be free: love cannot be compelled. He made us free so that He could love us and we could love Him in return. But free will also brings sin. *Freedom is the necessary prerequisite for virtue.* Coerced actions have no moral value.

Why does God mostly hide himself from us? *If He made his presence obvious, then humans would, in a sense, **be forced** to believe in Him.* Because His presence would be so overwhelming, even atheists would believe. And He wants us to believe of our own free will.

Why Me, Lord?

As a writer of little note, I don't have the nerve to say this about my own writing, but I am pleased that Pat Conroy (*Prince of Tides, Beach Music,* and my personal favorite, *The Great Santini,* etc.) did express it in an issue of *Writer* magazine.

> *A novel is my fingerprint, my identity card, and the writing of novels is one of the few ways I have found to approach the altar of God and creation itself. You try to worship God by performing the singular courageous and impossible favor of knowing yourself.*

Some of us were brought up to believe politics and religion were not proper topics for group discussion. I beg to differ. How can we learn if we don't openly discuss? I received several copies of an e-mail titled *Look Up.* It says in part, *Sorrow looks back, worry looks around, but faith looks up. Live simply, love generously, care deeply, speak kindly, and trust in our Creator—Who loves us.* I see myself as functionally illiterate on the subject of religion and faith. My bet is there are a lot of you out there in the boat with me. So I write not as an expert, but as someone with a deep desire to learn. I apologize to all you biblical scholars, evangelists, pastors, priests, and other preachers out there.

When I was a boy, religion in our home was tender to the touch, sometimes maybe even raw. Our forays into organized religion were subject to fits and starts. I heard a lot about a vengeful God from hellfire and brimstone preachers. I feared His wrath, and knew with some degree of certainty that I deserved it. My parents lost three of their six children. And it never (well, almost never) rained from the time I was six until I was twelve. As I watched our crops and cattle suffer and our pools dry up and our financial predicament regress from poor to desperate, I wondered what we had done to deserve such punishment. And were our neighbors also guilty of making God angry?

I described one of our sporadic embraces of religious fervor in a tent revival scene in *Rivers Flow*.

> *One man seated in the back of the tent bolted from*
> *his seat and ran down the aisle.... the man's tongue*
> *shot out of his mouth and flopped on his chin. He fell*
> *backward as if pulled by an invisible rope, flopping on*
> *his back and grinding his body against the grass. Jake*
> *could smell the dust and the bruised goat weeds the*
> *man was wallowing in.*

We were believers, but family tragedy and extreme hardship made religion uncomfortable to talk about. We simply did not understand. My Sunday School lessons began to take on some minor degree of clarity when Aunt Lilas gave me her son Jerry's set of children's Bibles when Jerry left for the service (both Testaments in color and pictures). I still occasionally refer to them.

During a motivational seminar more than twenty years ago, I was asked to name the times in my life when I reached a pinnacle of achievement in any task, no matter how small; times when I had been in what athletes call the zone; when I had done something well beyond my perceived capabilities. I couldn't name a single one at the time, but they began to come to me later. I read *Flow: The Psychology of Optimal Achievement* and began to understand. But only when I started writing and making flow a theme for four novels did I see that achieving the pinnacle called flow or zone comes only when we are one with the Holy Trinity. It usually comes when we are deeply engaged in some type of mental or physical endeavor that requires intense focus and creativity and when we are being of service to others. Flow is God's presence talking to us, loving us.

As I grew older and tried to build and fortify a belief system that would set the course for the remainder of my life, I examined the primary principles Christians must accept, believe, and *understand*. I was a "show me" kind of person. Even a person of weak faith (as I was) can hardly deny that Jesus Christ changed the course of human history more than any human before or since. And He did it in a short lifespan without traveling very far from home.

Considering those facts, a logical thinker has to accept that a higher power had to be involved and the Immaculate Conception, Crucifixion, and Resurrection became easier to accept as possibilities. But to my everlasting shame, I could not get my logical brain around how and why Jesus died for our sins and how His Crucifixion forever affected all of our lives. One preacher corrected me when I referred to Jesus as a human, saying He was God. True, but He was also human.

He ate, tired, slept, hurt and bled. But why? And why did He ask God to take away the extreme pain He knew was in store (*"remove this cup from me"*) before He was put on the cross? I could not reconcile that with an all-powerful being. That opened the door for C. S. Lewis to explain it was because He was human. Makes sense now, but I could not see the logic in it for a long time.

Although tens of thousands of books and millions of words have been written on religion, spirituality and faith by scholars and experts, there are still many who have questions they are afraid or ashamed to ask, doubts they dare not express. Writing about these things may help them, and it will almost certainly help me.

As I was refining the pages of this section, I received the following message by e-mail from Dr. Charles Stanley's *In Touch Ministries* magazine. It said, "Don't discredit yourself or count yourself out. You can walk through the open doors God has placed before you and have a significant part in reaching the world with the good news of Christ." I saw that as reason enough to push on.

I do ask God to inspire my written and spoken words. Then I ask myself, "Who am I to ask such a thing? Why would God choose me?" During quiet times, I hear the answer, "Because you asked."

So does that mean all of my writings have been divinely inspired? The obvious answer seems to be a resounding no. Okay then, which ones, which books, which articles might have been inspired? And why are inspired words all mixed up with my own inferior human efforts? Are there just a few paragraphs of inspired words mixed in with the millions of words I have written?

The only answer that comes close to satisfying my need for clarity is that God is teaching me as I go along, and I am certainly not, and likely never will be, a finished product until the end. *He who began a good work in you will carry it on to completion* (Phillipians 1:6, NIV). Allowing me, even encouraging me to write and occasionally throwing in a little divine inspiration is His way of teaching me.

So how does this inspiration come? Do I hear God's voice? Do I see visions? No, at least not in the normal senses of sight and sound. I do believe, however, that God speaks to me often, just as He does to everyone else who asks to hear His message. Guidance may come in a dream, a random thought, a phone call, a chance encounter with a stranger, a passage in a book, an assigned chore, a conversation with a loved one, a book that drops off the shelf at the right time, or in any one of hundreds of ways.

I have traveled down a lot of blind alleys, taken wrong paths, failed many times, and hurt others by my actions. When I drove life's car into the ditch, somehow I learned from the mistake and got back on the road again. Sören Kierkegaard said of such occasions,

> *The true significance of what happened would*
> *inevitably become clear to me and I would be numb*
> *with surprise: I have done many things in my life*
> *that conflict with the great aims I set for myself and*
> *something has always set me on the true path again.*

The mistakes I made helped me to develop a belief system, a set of principles to live by. Yes, I still veer from those principles, still occasionally amend them, but I never abandon them. I ask for forgiveness and get back on the right path.

My life has undoubtedly been blessed. Prayers have been answered. I am ashamed to admit that, for the most part, I neither properly recognized nor expressed gratitude for such blessings until long after they were received. More often than not, I did not even recognize the blessings when I received them. Why? Because they seldom came on the timetable I requested, and usually not in the way I expected. More often than not, I attributed the blessing to my own personal efforts. And yet, I was forgiven for my ingratitude. And that defines God's grace.

How were my eyes opened? More than thirty years ago, I began writing. At first, it was just a journal, then essays about my private feelings, nothing for public consumption. Then I began writing for lectures, seminars and workshops. The writing caused me to reflect, to look back, to be still and listen. Psalms 46:10: *Be still, and know that I am God,* took on new meaning for me.

So how does God speak to me? His voice sometimes comes to my mind as clearly expressed thoughts. I used to half-seriously ask, "God, could you please deliver your inspiration at more convenient times—like when I have pen and paper handy, or when I'm not driving or dozing off at night?" Those requests entered my mind involuntarily, because even I knew better than to question an inspired gift from the Almighty. But one night, quite unexpectedly, God answered. "I have repeatedly asked you to be still, to be quiet, to clear your cluttered mind, but you have ignored Me. So I take opportunities as they present themselves. By the way, a thank you might be nice."

I got the message. Some of you are probably thinking I am hearing what I want to hear. Others are saying these words are only my imagination at work. Right on both counts. I do want to hear it. But sometimes, I hear things I really don't want to hear. And, I believe that my imagination (subconscious, if you will), is God speaking through The Holy Spirit, in language I can clearly understand. That is what I call faith.

As I read the words above, they still seem arrogant, self-serving. Why me? What qualifies this sinner, this man who ignored blessings when they were received because I could not be still long enough to recognize them? My answer: Why not me? Why not you? I used to envy those with invincible, unwavering, lifelong faith, the preachers who seem to have all the answers. Mine has been a meandering search along a path littered with doubt, even cynicism. My saving grace is that I never stopped searching. I just looked in a lot of wrong places.

In the final pages of this book, I will try to detail the wrong and right paths I followed and how I tried to find answers to questions that kept me from building my faith. I still occasionally struggle with these questions as life's paths lead in directions I never expected, but I have learned how to deal with them.

Try me, Lord, if you think there's a way
I can try to repay all I've taken from you
Maybe Lord, I can show someone else
What I've been through myself, on my way back to you
—Kris Kristofferson

*Sometimes our light goes out but is blown again
into flame by an encounter with another human being.
Each of us owes the deepest thanks to those
who have rekindled this inner light.*

—Albert Schweitzer

Self-Help vs. God's Help

Many religious leaders scoff and express disdain for the "self-help" shelves in bookstores, explaining that real answers to the most important life questions can only be found in the religious section. They are right on some level. However, self-help gurus and their books, seminars, and recorded messages provided a gateway to the religious section for me. I deeply immersed myself into a world where prayers are called affirmations; where the subconscious is recognized, but not as a deity; a world where God and The Holy Trinity are seldom or never mentioned but "invisible forces" and "the powers of the universe" are. The teachers in that world made religious writings easier to understand, easier to see their practical applications to my life. I later learned many of my mentors in that world were, in fact, biblical scholars who saw themselves as providing a portal for skeptics like me to enter into a more spiritual world, the world of faith. I was just late.

I told a college graduating class to seek wisdom wherever you can find it, excluding neither the self-help nor religious sections. And please do not exclude the ancient texts or wise people just because they might have lived centuries ago. And don't adopt a rigorous requirement that any principle must be supported by the latest scientific findings. Science has been wrong many times on many subjects for long periods of time throughout history—often on purpose when money and power interfere. But if science is your only belief system, then look at several scientific studies and books about NDE's (Near-Death Experiences) by Paul Perry, Raymond Moody, MD, PhD and Jeffrey Long, MD. The evidence of an afterlife in their voluminous research and many books is ample.

The Bible is filled with stories and examples of God's awesome power. These stories have been told for centuries. When I talk with non-believers, I ask if there are not at least two or three miracles they could consider believing. If they can't accept He raised humans from the dead, healed the sick and afflicted; then, how about feeding four thousand with seven loaves and a few small fish, maybe feeding five thousand with five loaves and two fish? Does the fact these miracles were witnessed by thousands and have endured for centuries impress you at all?

Doubts and questions plagued my own meandering journey toward faith. I have often imagined what God might say if He were telling the story of my life. "When he was a boy, he saw Me as vengeful and angry because of what he heard from others and what happened in his own family. He was frightened of Me. As a young man, he was weak, sinful, and cynical. In middle age, he wanted to live a good life, be a better man, and have a strong faith, but he still did not understand. He diligently searched for answers to the questions that plagued him, 'Why am I here? Am I doing what I am supposed to do?' He looked in some wrong places, came to some wrong conclusions, but I had patience and forgave him because he was trying very, very hard, and because I love him. In old age, he walked through the doors I had always left open for him, studied my words, and came to Me. He began to understand I am a God of love, not vengeance."

It is not so true that "prayer changes things"
as that prayer changes me and I change things.
God has so constituted things that prayer on the basis of
Redemption alters the way in which a man looks at things.
Prayer is not a question of altering things externally,
but of working wonders in a man's disposition.
—Oswald Chambers

*I have done many things in my life that conflict
with the great aims I set for myself and "something"
has always set me on the true path again.*

—Sören Kierkegaard

Free Will vs. God's Will

How many of us have heard a tragedy or untimely death explained as "God's will." I still struggle with this one. I think it's because I have spent the better part of my life believing in personal responsibility and that seems to run counter to the idea of "God's will." Some believe in predestination (fate)—that God has planned each of our lives in advance. I have always believed in free will. If we don't have choices, how can we earn our eternal rewards?

A recent unattributed article says,

> The Potter has power over the clay. He can do what
> He chooses. We humans do have limited free will,
> but God's will is greater. So even if we try to resist
> His sculpting hand, He continues to work toward His
> purpose. The master Craftsman has set out to achieve
> a particular design in us, and He has a plan to make
> it take shape.

I don't disagree with that, but it leaves questions unanswered and confuses me a little. Since His will is greater, will He shape us all to His purpose, no matter how much we resist?

I think not. Otherwise, we're all going to heaven. The author goes on to say,

> ...human clay sometimes shifts off-center and becomes misshapen. Just as clay can be fashioned only when it sits precisely in the middle of the wheel, Christians must be in the Father's will to grow spiritually. The Potter maneuvers the drifting believer back into position and begins remolding. He never discards His vessels but tirelessly works to perfect them.

I think the key words here are, "*Christians must be in the Father's will to grow spiritually*" and "*He never discards his vessels.*" I believe God has a will for each of us, but we must try to continually return to the "*middle of the wheel*," and we must do that through asking for His guidance. If not, we will get misshapen and stay that way. One pastor believes there is a difference between God's *determined* will and His *desired* will. That speaks to me. Certain things are going to happen because God has ordained them; He wants other things to happen, but they will only if we hold up our end.

I still have to remind myself daily to let go and let God. I have trouble surrendering, because there are so many days when I am still unsure if I am doing what God intends for me to do. Surrendering is not giving up or letting life carry us along on *any wind that blows*. Letting go means having faith; trying to live our lives according to God's teachings; asking for forgiveness when we fail; using the gifts God gave each of us; and asking for guidance to fulfill our reason for being—our purpose in life. When we are confused, we must believe, pray, and just do the things that come into our minds. When we are unsure if we are doing the right things, we must believe. We must have faith that we are being guided, that even if we do not understand today, we will understand tomorrow, next week, or next year. We must keep taking the steps our conscience tells us to take.

Even though I can look back on my life and see example after example of His guidance, I have to remind myself daily to have faith, ask, and then surrender. If I do those things, He will help me to apply my particular gifts to the highest possible purpose for me. He will bring the circumstances, events, and people into my life to bring about His will for me. And I have to accept I may not understand what has happened until I look back. Again, life is lived forward, but understood backward.

I still ask myself about the times when I did, spoke, thought, or wrote the wrong things. Who inspired those times? Where was God? Where was my faith? Writing and the reflection necessary for writing helped me to understand those times. My selfish nature had allowed me to take credit for every success and blame circumstances or others for every failure. I let ego take control. When I intensified my search for answers, when I accepted with certainty there are forces in the universe much more powerful than us mortals (even though I gave those forces wrong identities at first), I was rewarded through grace. My mistakes happened because I did not fervently ask for God's guidance in making decisions, in achieving what I wanted, charging on, thinking I was fully capable of taking care of it myself. I did not meditate, get still, and listen.

*A man is never so tall
as when he is on his knees.*

—Alice von Hildebrand

How and Why Do We Pray?

I can't answer that question, of course. Each of us must find what works for us. As a child, I was often embarrassed by public prayer. I feared raising my head or opening my eyes at the wrong time. My first reading of scripture in a children's Bible gave me comfort.

> But when you pray, go into your room, close the door
> and pray to your Father, who is unseen. Then your
> Father, Who sees what is done in secret, will reward you.
> —Matthew 6:6

I felt redeemed and determined all public prayer was somehow misguided. I no longer think that, but still believe private prayer is what we need most.

I was also plagued with the questions most of us wrestle with. Is it wrong to ask for material rewards or success in our careers, for example? One pastor writes our prayers should be more about what He wills than what we want. I find that advice confusing, especially if one is unsure of God's will for our lives. I prefer to turn it around and ask for guidance, faith and strength to conform my desires to His will. And I ask for help in my continued quest to build invincible, impenetrable, unwavering faith so that I can surrender and know that God will use me to carry out His will for my life, to help me achieve my reason for being. And I try to remember to express gratitude for God's patience, love and forgiveness in every prayer.

Something I read or heard influenced me to concentrate on one day at a time instead of a lifetime before and ahead and to use these steps:

1. Give thanks for yesterday's blessings. Even after a terrible day, there is always at least one reason to be grateful.
2. Ask forgiveness for yesterday's sins.
3. Ask for blessings for others today (be specific).
4. Ask for blessings for yourself today (be specific).
5. Ask for spiritual discernment so that you can hear and understand God's voice and understand His will for your life.
6. Surrender, be quiet, and listen.

I have read many articles on the subject of prayer, tried various methods of prayerful meditation, failed many times at finding the right words and thoughts. I have written many prayers, copied many from other sources, and memorized many lines.

> When you pray, don't babble on and on as people of
> other religions do. They think their prayers are answered
> only by repeating their words again and again.
> —Matthew 6:7

Do not be quick with your mouth, do not be hasty in
your heart to utter anything before God. God is in
heaven and you are on earth, so let your words be few.
—Ecclesiastes 5:2

Still, I think writing the best words I could create or copy
from more learned sources helped me. I wanted my prayers
to say what was in my heart and I needed a pen and paper
and keyboard to refine exactly what I needed to express in
my prayers. Over a period of several years, I have refined (and
memorized) my prayers, so that I will not leave anything out
I need to say. Trying to be eloquent in thought or voice at
prayer time without that crutch sometimes caused my mind
to wander, my memory to fail, or my tongue to tie itself in
knots. I don't believe God expects eloquence, but seeking the
right words helps me to give voice or thought to daily prayers
that don't confuse me or make my mind wander. I still make
mental and physical notes of people or events I need to pray
about. And now that I have what I think are the best words
at my disposal, I seldom recite the memorized prayer because
the process of writing it helped me to feel as if I can open a
thought or verbal dialogue with God more easily.

I try to be worthy of a relationship with the Holy Spirit
filled with love and forgiveness. That is what I want and what
I believe God wants. I also believe we must schedule a time
and place regularly and often, or else the relationship will
suffer.

Does God answer? Maybe not how or when we want Him
to, but yes, He does. I try to see His face in the eyes of good
people and animals, my loved ones, in clouds; to feel His touch
in the kiss of a raindrop or snowflake, the soft embrace of a

gentle breeze; hear His voice in the roll of thunder or a bird's song. I don't hear a booming voice, but I do hear thoughts and I do see signs, especially when I pay attention with an air of expectancy and faith. I try to remember I am not Moses or Paul. Remember what was asked of them when God revealed himself to them?

Does prayer work? Yes. For me, it helps to solve one of the most difficult parts of the Christian life—letting go and surrendering to God's will without knowing for sure what God's will for my life is. Prayer helps me to continually recognize surrendering does not mean abdication of responsibility. Instead, it means acceptance of the even greater responsibility to carry out God's will for my life. I still sometimes have to suppress the urge to take charge, to take full responsibility and credit for what happens. Prayer strengthens my faith, helps me to surrender and to understand better how the Holy Spirit works in my life.

Do we need to be on our knees? If it works, then do it. A submissive posture works best for me. It helps me to focus and concentrate and it conveys respect and love. Of course, many pray just fine lying, sitting or standing. Where do we need to pray? Anyplace will do, but I like a completely dark closet to help me focus. I can't recall where I read them or who said them, but these words helped.

> *The Holy Spirit prays with us and for us. We do not pray alone. Regular prayer helps us to bask in the presence of the Holy Spirit, to become closer and more intimate with God, to better understand the Trinity and why Jesus left the Holy Spirit with us.*

The Bible
in a Few Words

As a layperson and admitted functional illiterate on Scripture, I began (embarrassingly late in life) a study of both Testaments. Oh, I read children's versions of both when I was young and have sporadically read at both as an adult. I bought and read many short-cut books to learn about the Bible when I became frustrated with reading actual Scripture I found confusing. And I don't just mean archaic language. I tried several translated, simplified versions.

I was confused by what seemed to be contradictions between what God said vs. what He did, especially in the Old Testament. I was also confused by timelines, i.e. when did this happen? Why are both Testaments not presented in chronological order? Why do the same people have different names? Why are the same stories told by different people? And why does God do things in the Old Testament that seem to defy the teachings in the New Testament? I even embarked on several suggested Bible study courses, reading certain passages on consecutive days. It didn't work for me.

So I decided to read both Testaments from start to finish. My sense-of-order brain insisted, of course, that I start with the Old Testament. Lots of people have many different ways to learn. I have learned what does and does not work for me. This approach made sense to me. Although it seemed sort of sacrilegious at first, I highlighted and made margin notes in the Bibles on this reading journey. I read consistently and I read for fairly long sittings. That helped.

I kept a small notebook beside my reading chair and made notes of the various passages that had always confused or interested me—passages related to the Holy Spirit, The Holy Trinity, how to pray, why bad things happen, why and how the Crucifixion and Resurrection paid for our sins, baptism, finding life's purpose, the afterlife, Satan and hell, etc.

I also found passages and characters in the Bible that I had never noticed before. Melchizedek, for example—who is this man who had the power to bless and minister to Abram (Abraham) and whom Abram gave a tithe? I breezed right by him in my first reading, thinking he was just one more hard-to-pronounce name in a long line of kings and prophets. But I noticed him in the second reading (see how rereading increases comprehension?). I found him in Genesis, Hebrews, and Psalms. He was King of Salem, from which Jerusalem was named. Salem also means peace. David said, "*Thou art a priest forever after the order of Melchizedek.*" It was also said that he was "*without mother, without father, without descent.*" What does that mean? I found myself starting to read Scripture like a novel.

And who was the *beloved* disciple, the one referred to in John as the "*one Jesus loved*"? Exploring the answer to these and other mysteries made things much more interesting.

I stuck to my disciplined approach through three readings of both Testaments in three different versions. It took me a little over two years. I have started the fourth read. This time, I am rereading the New International Version Student Bible. So, do I consider myself now educated on Scripture? Sorry, but no. Reading the Bible three times made me realize I have only scratched the surface of understanding. Yet, I am not discouraged. Just the opposite. For the scratch I have made offers the richest bounty life has to offer. I have learned a lot, developed a lot of questions, and the reading goes much faster now and my comprehension rate is going up exponentially.

Of course, there is the distinct possibility my interpretation of what I am reading is very flawed. On second thought, there is little doubt that it is probably flawed, but is it totally wrong? Several ministers certainly disagree with my opinions (or I disagree with theirs). But then again, reading has brought me the comfort of allowing myself to refine my own belief system with each reread. I believe God is okay with that, as long as I grasp the essentials. I reconciled (mostly) the seeming contradictions in the Old Testament by listening closely to explanations and researching what others have written about the subjects.

When I switched from nonfiction to fiction writing, I was introduced to loglines, book jacket summaries, and synopses. A logline (sometimes called an elevator speech) is a one sentence description of the book you have written. A book jacket summary is a few lines printed on the inside flap of a book jacket meant to entice readers. In this age of digital printing, such summaries are even shorter and are printed on the back of the book. Imagine reducing 100,000 words to 100 words that will persuade a reader to buy and read the book. A synopsis is a summary (usually 250 to 500 words) that tells the entire story of a novel. We reduce four hundred or so pages to one or two. Synopses are usually required by potential agents and publishers. I find these things very difficult to write, especially for character-driven novels.

But as I started my third read, I started to imagine what a logline or synopsis for the Bible would be like. How would I explain the Old and New Testament if I were forced to reduce each to a few paragraphs? Should we even try to do that? I, for one, need that type of thing firmly in my mind so the details will come easier. I prayed for forgiveness as I tried to do it.

The Old Testament in Three Paragraphs

God makes man in His own image and gives Him free will and almost complete freedom. He places Adam and Eve in a world of beauty and almost perfect peace and harmony where they want for nothing. He promises them dominion over every living thing on Earth. They only have to follow a few simple rules (some would say one rule, but I believe there were at least two). But they disobey and mankind keeps disobeying for about fifteen hundred years, until finally God can find only one righteous man on earth. He sends the Great Flood to destroy humanity except for Noah and his family. After the flood, descendants of Noah populate the earth and the great biblical stories and characters evolve. God promises a childless and old Abraham he will be the father of many kings and nations. God continually shows His power and asks only that mankind have faith and know that He is God. Over a thousand years after the flood, He sends Moses to lead the Israelites out of slavery in Egypt. When ten plagues and the awesome power of God finally force the pharaoh to accede to

Moses' plea to let His people go, Moses leads his people out of
Egypt and slavery (The Exodus). God parts the Red Sea and
drowns the pursuing army.

With clouds during the day and pillars of fire by night,
He leads his chosen people toward the Promised Land and to
freedom. He feeds them with manna from the sky. Yet, after all
these miracles, many still do not believe, proving that impres-
sive displays of God's power will not guarantee faith and many
humans are short-term thinkers with a "What have you done
for me lately?" attitude. Approximately 430 years after his covenant with Abraham, God delivers the Ten Commandments
and other laws through Moses, but Moses discovers the people
have created things to worship while he was on the mountain rather than worshiping the Creator. After forty years in
the wilderness and because they continually disobeyed and
showed lack of faith, only two Israelites over the age of twenty,
(Joshua and Caleb—not even Moses) crossed the Jordan into
the Promised Land.

For fourteen hundred more years, God's chosen people
engage in wars with the tribes of the Promised Land. They
experience many defeats, many victories. They lose and regain
God's Temple and the Ark of the Covenant, become oppres-
sors and oppressed. They ask for a king to lead them, and God
gives them Saul. Saul's reign is a failure, but he is followed
by David and Solomon who restore the Temple and return
the Ark. For over nine hundred more years, a succession of
kings leads the Jews into and away from idolatry, slavery and
power. Great prophets such as Elijah, Elisha, Isaiah, Jeremiah,
Ezekiel, and Daniel continue to bring God's message to His
chosen people and to their kings.

The New Testament in Three Paragraphs

The Old Testament has many prophesies of the coming of Jesus. God knows His creations will continue to sin and lack faith, that no human will follow rules perfectly, and all who try will ultimately fail. Twenty-five hundred years after the flood, John the Baptist is born to prepare the way for Jesus. A short while later, Jesus, a descendant of David the giant slayer and a King in the Old Testament, is born. At approximately thirty, Jesus puts down His tools, walks away from His father's carpentry shop and begins His ministry. He is baptized by his cousin John the Baptist and gathers the disciples. For the next three years, He heals the sick, raises the dead, speaks in parables, and delivers the most important sermons of all time to multitudes. There are no miracles on a massive scale, just enough positive demonstrations of His power to spread the Word. He asks only one thing—*Believe in Me and in my Father.* It is said that He never travels more than two-hundred miles from his home, yet He changes the world in ways not seen before or since, has a greater effect on mankind than all the kings, emperors, warriors and scholars who came before or after. He is God in human form, the Christ, the Messiah, yet He comes in humility and lives His life as a servant. He takes Peter, James, and John, His closest disciples, to a high mountain where He is transfigured *(and He was transfigured before them, and His face shone like the sun, and His garments turned white as the light itself).* Moses and Elijah appeared by His side and God's voice thundered from heaven, *"This is my beloved son, in whom I am well pleased."*

Jesus joins the procession to Jerusalem for Passover but stops in Bethany to raise His good friend and follower Lazarus from the dead. Because He is a threat to the establishment

Jews, He is nailed to a cross between two thieves. He endures the most agonizing of deaths and suffers in ways only humans can to prove He is human. Then, in the greatest miracle of all, He rises from death, proving He is also God. He reveals himself to his disciples and a few others and gives them further instructions on how to spread His Word, the Good News that is the Gospel. Forty days later, He ascends into Heaven, leaving behind The Holy Spirit to dwell within us and with us, to comfort us and guide us, and leaving a pathway for weak mankind to sin again and be forgiven. We only have to have faith, ask for forgiveness, and believe. This is the New Covenant, a covenant destined to last forever. He leaves us with the greatest commandments saying,

> *Love the Lord your God with all your heart and with all your soul and with all your mind. Love your neighbor as yourself. All the Law and the Prophets hang on these two commandments.*

He instructs His disciples to teach all nations to observe His commandments. The disciples, and later Paul and others, go forth and continue to tell and write the story of Jesus. Finally, in Revelation, a man named John writes of visions he has while imprisoned in an Alcatraz-like Roman prison on a rocky island called Patmos. Because his visions are filled with symbols, grand imagery, and unique numbers, they have been subject to many conflicting theories as to their exact meaning. But there is little doubt the writer named John who was being persecuted for his Christian beliefs was revealing his visions of the cosmic significance of the return of Jesus Christ when followers of Christ will be made safe at last.

Oversimplified, even flippant? Guilty. I needed simplicity to help me study the details, the many stories, parables, prophets and kings, famines and wars that surround and support this basic premise for me. The confusion I had when I read the Old Testament gained clarity as I sorted out the differences between the Old Covenant and the New Covenant. One was a covenant that killed and the other gave life. One was a covenant written in stone, the other written on the heart of man. When I become confused, I go back to this summary. You should try doing your own synopses. They would undoubtedly be different than mine. By the time this is printed, I will have probably changed my own several times. The more I study the Bible, the more books written about Christianity by true Bible and religious scholars mean to me.

Belief does not claim that we should know anything about the furniture in heaven or the temperature of hell, or to be too certain about any details of the kingdom of God in which history is consummated.

—Reinhold Niebuhr

Final Thoughts

Frederick Buechner's memoir, *Telling Secrets*, sat on my books-to-read shelf for a long time, possibly a decade. I don't recall why or when I bought it and can't explain why I never read it until recently. Maybe it was waiting until I needed it. Maybe it was one of those times when inspiration comes when we need it most. This book did literally drop to the floor when I was rearranging a shelf. That happens a lot.

The book is difficult to describe. The author is an ordained minister who writes fiction and nonfiction. This memoir is in three parts. The titles seem allegorical, but Buechner delves into very real, personal and tragic events in his life which I won't spoil here. Even if his stories had not worked for me (which they did), these quotes made the book one I will never forget.

As a writer, this was a favorite gem.

> ... *a book you write, like a dream you dream, can
> have more healing and truth and wisdom in it at least
> for yourself than you feel in any way responsible for.*

I especially liked the author's open, almost self-deprecating style, not what we usually expect from an ordained minister.

As a husband, father and grandfather, I also enjoyed the way he integrated the meetings of a particular group to bring readers a valuable lesson. Buechner does not mention the group by name, but you will recognize it when he eloquently describes their meetings.

> *They have slogans, which you can either dismiss*
> *as hopelessly simplistic or cling on to like driftwood*
> *in a stormy sea. One of them is 'Let Go and Let*
> *God'—which is so easy to say and for people like me,*
> *so far from easy to follow. Stop trying to protect, to*
> *rescue, to judge, to manage the lives around you—*
> *your children's lives, the lives of your husband, your*
> *wife, your friends—because that is just what you are*
> *powerless to do. Leave it to God. It is an astonishing*
> *thought. It can be a life-transforming thought.*

And as a believer, this is my favorite:

> *Even if there be no hereafter, I would live my time*
> *believing in a grand thing that ought to be true if it*
> *is not. . . . I will go farther, and say I would rather*
> *die forevermore believing as Jesus believed, than live*
> *forevermore believing as those who deny him.*

NOTE FROM AUTHOR: The original manuscript ended here. But on the day after I made the final changes, I went for a morning horseback ride to have coffee with friends. On the way back, I found two sheets of paper in the ditch across the road from my old friend and mentor Dr. Fred Tarpley's house. His redwood house sits way back in the woods like a reclusive author or professor's should (Fred was the opposite of reclusive) but not so far that I could not see two large dumpsters appear in his yard a few weeks after he died. I don't know what is in them, but I suspect a lot of Fred's research and books had to be discarded. Many had suffered water damage and fire damage when his house caught fire many years ago.

When I saw the yellowed and tattered sheets, I immediately thought of Fred. The wind had probably carried them out of the dumpster, across the road and into my horseback path that particular morning. The two sheets of paper were printed on both sides and I could tell from the missing page numbers they had been part of a book or manual for teachers in a religion course of some kind. A date in the margin told me they were printed more than half a century ago.

If you read my notes at the beginning and got this far, you know I struggled with the last part of this book. As I said in the opening notes, I struggled to write about things very personal to me and to offer opinions on subjects I may be unqualified to write about. I considered deleting the last section of the book many times. I was still considering deleting it when I dismounted and picked up the sheets. I found these words:

> If Christianity does not begin with the individual, it
> does not begin; but if it ends with the individual, it ends.

I had particular problems with the "How to Pray" section, because I am still figuring it out. In the yellowed, tattered sheets, I found these words:

> God hears the meditations of our hearts, rather than
> the words of our mouths. If we pray one way with our
> lips and another with our true feelings, which is the
> true prayer?

I might be making too much of what may be a coincidence, but if I have learned anything in this life, it is to pay attention and to engage in deliberate practice of the things we want to get better at. God sends signals we may miss if we are not paying attention. Finding those two pages told me to leave the last section in.

In his book *Letters to My Son*, Kent Nerbern says,

> *Once you love an art enough that you can be taken up in it, you are able to experience an echo of the great creative act that mysteriously has given life to us all. It may be the closest any of us can get to God. Spiritual growth is honed and perfected only through practice. Like an instrument, it must be played. Like a path, it must be walked. Whether through prayer or meditation or worship or good works, you must move yourself in the direction of spiritual betterment . . . only a fool refuses to walk in the sunlight because he cannot see the shape of the sun.*

This has been my effort to walk in the sunlight. What more can I say? Thanks. It's been quite a ride.

I guess grace doesn't have to be logical.
If it did, it wouldn't be grace. It's not every day
that you find someone who will give you a second chance,
much less someone who will give you a second chance every day.
—Max Lucado

Now, a few of the many memories left behind by

MARION SHEPHERD AINSWORTH

*This is a story that happened
more than four decades ago.*

The Night They Bolted

I think they were a matched pair of Belgian mares, but they might have been Percheron geldings. Seems that my cousin Marion owned a pair of each breed at one time or another. He used to drive them by Mother's house on Dogtown Road when he was breaking them to a sled.

What I do remember is the night they bolted as we approached a deep creek. It might have been the squirrel that ran between their legs or the screech of that owl that flew over, but I think it was the noise of the wagon they thought was chasing them.

It was their first time to pull a wagon; it was dark, and they imagined the strange loud contraption behind them was in pursuit and about to run over them. The faster they ran, the faster it ran. We had pulled off the asphalt highway to cut down on the noise the wagon wheels made, but that left us with no barrier to the deep creek.

We were pretty confident they would stop when they saw the big drop-off, but it was very dark, and we had to consider the consequences if they didn't see the creek. The wagon would likely turn end over end and land on one or both of us, not to mention what the wreck would do to the horses. And the horses and wagon were prized possessions for my cousin.

Marion stood on the foot brake and pulled back on the reins with all his might. I grabbed one rein and tried to turn one of their heads. But the pulls were a minor nuisance compared to the pair's terror of the contraption chasing them. They never slowed; they ran faster. Marion shouted through the wind. "Jump!"

I couldn't believe my ears. The wagon was traveling as fast as panicked horses can run. I looked at the horses' bobbing heads and pinned ears, at the fast approaching creek, and back at Marion. The expression on his face said he meant it. I shook my head. "I ain't goin' unless you do."

He shouted through the din. "Go out the back. I'll keep trying to stop 'em or get 'em back on the road until you're off, then I'll jump before we go in the creek."

I looked at the fast-moving dirt and weeds as I lay on my belly and hung my legs out the back. I thought I might be able to hit the ground running and avoid falling if I could get up to speed quickly enough—a foolish notion. I decided to wait until the last minute to jump.

But the grass and dirt turned to asphalt as Marion turned one runaway's head enough to bring the wagon back on the road. It leaned on two wheels as it left the ditch and loosened my tenuous grip on the wagon bed. Any choice about jumping was gone.

I slid along the pavement on my belly. Back on the road, the horses saw the bridge rails and stopped just about the time I stopped sliding. Marion stood on the spring seat and looked back at me. He later said I looked like a hobo thumbing a ride. The outer layer of skin was gone from my palms and little spots of blood appeared around embedded gravel and splinters from the wagon bed.

The leather was shredded from my new leather-covered belt buckle and my front belt loops were missing. The knees of my jeans were torn out and my shirt cuffs were strings of thread. My denim jacket protected the shirt snaps, but they were all undone. The toes of my boots had taken the worst of it, but all in all, I felt pretty good as I stood and found nothing broken.

It was a cool fall night, and I was happy to be able to walk, happy the horses and Marion were unhurt. I got back in the wagon and we drove the horses to the barn without any more trouble.

Marion's wife Pat was waiting at Aunt Hildred's (Marion's mother). Pat scolded him. "You might have been hurt real bad." He consoled her and winked at me as he told her there had been no real danger.

I must have been quite a sight with ragged jeans and shirt and the hide gone from my palms as I stood to leave. "I think he was trying to get rid of me." Pretty soon, we were all laughing.

A few days later, we drove those green-broke horses into town for a parade. We stopped at Chute 1, my western wear and tack store, put the store banner on the wagon, and rode in a big homecoming parade. It was biting cold and the wind got up just after the parade, but we drove them the seven or so miles back to Shiloh in the teeth of that wind. We were chilled to the bone. Aunt Hildred's coffee never tasted so good and we took a rare afternoon nap on the floor beside her stove.

Shep and I had many adventures like that. We took a mule-drawn covered wagon and five horses across Texas to prove our mettle to our fathers and grandfather who had made the same trip eighty years earlier. We participated in a roundup on a famous Texas ranch. Mostly though, we commiserated, laughed a lot, and shared our joys and miseries. By the way, if he were here now, he could tell us the breed, sex and the names of those two runaway horses.

I stop at his little tire shop almost every time I drive into Cooper. I don't recall the last time I bought tires anywhere else. I roll down the window to better let the memories wash over me. I usually choke up a little, do a little salute. Then I hear his strong voice. "Go on now, Jim. Go on." The tone is like a command, so like Marion, a man with a strong voice.

After I finish my business in Cooper, I usually stop again, try to picture him sitting in that little office, surrounded by friends who dropped by every day to shoot the bull. I try to see him in the back, wrestling with a tractor tire men half his age and twice his size would have trouble handling.

This time, the voice is less stern, gentler, "It's all right, Jim. Go on now. You have to go on."

It all happened so fast. Seems like we found out he was sick one day and he was gone the next. It wasn't that fast, of course, but we didn't have time to get our arms around it. Course, no amount of time would have made us ready to let him go.

We're Not Done Yet

Those were the words I wrote inside the book when I gave a copy of *A River of Stories* to Marion Shepherd Ainsworth, my cousin and lifelong friend. I will never forget the day I laid the book *hot-off-the-press* on his knee and we both cried, knowing he might not live long enough to read it. He is mentioned multiple times in the book, because his life stories are threaded throughout my own. Soon after, he went to the hospital for the last time. Had he been well, he would have been one of the first to read the book. He read all my books and always called after turning the last page. After a little light-hearted teasing, he praised my words and told me what the book meant to him.

William Zinser said in *Writing About Your Life,* "to feel the intimacy of brothers is a marvelous thing in life." Marion and I were not brothers, but our fathers were—and our mothers were sisters. Unless you've been one, you may not understand double cousins. We have the same bloodlines, the same aunts and uncles, the same cousins, the same grandparents, the same great-grandparents and so on. Marion's family and mine were like siblings without the squabbles and rivalry.

When my brother Eddy was killed in a plane crash at thirty-four, Marion came to me and said, "I never had a brother. You don't have one now. I know I will never be Eddy, but I would like to be your brother." I knew that offer came from his heart.

Of course, I had always thought of Marion more as a brother than cousin, but I came to appreciate what he said more and more as the years went by. He gets more credit for that than I do. He made sure the ties that bound us never frayed. Whenever there was a death in the family, a setback, or a loss of any kind, Marion and I gathered like lost sheep. The bond developed in childhood grew stronger.

We were as different as daylight and dark, but as alike as two peas in a pod. People usually said we were a pair of throwbacks, born a hundred years too late, and I guess they were right. We shared a fascination with our ancestors, loved old stories, cowboys and the western way of life. We tested each other's memories about past events and people. I might know more about things that took place long before we were born, but he knew more about things that happened during our lifetimes. When I wrote about the past, he was one my most reliable sources of information. He had a great memory for names and places because, I think, people just interested him. He loved his family and his fellow man—and he loved stories.

In time-honored Texas tradition, I called him by both his given names, Marion Shepherd. Sometimes I called him Shep because that's what Daddy called him. He called me Jimmy Hiram (Horn or Harm). When I heard him call my names, it always took me back for a few seconds to my youth, made me feel connected to him, to our families, and to our shared history. Because he was a lover of stories and jokes and laughter in general, he acquired an extra nickname of Dabo, presumably given to him by my brother before either of them could really talk. It stuck for the remainder of his life because it seemed to fit.

Not only did Marion and I enjoy a shared family history, we also shared many adventures together, mostly due to his adventurous spirit. Delivering his eulogy to a filled church in 2014, I told the story of how one of our adventures began.

Back in 1997, he proposed an outlandish plan to travel across Texas horseback with a mule-drawn covered wagon. He wanted to retrace the journey our parents and grandparents had made eighty years earlier. I don't have the words to explain the bizarre nature of that call. Let me just say it came within the only short window of time during my entire life when I would not have just laughed and declined. But he seemed to sense the window and was not surprised when I asked, "How soon can we get together the horses, mules, wagon and supplies and decide on the exact route they took back then?"

Neither of us owned a wagon or mules at the time. Marion didn't even own a horse. He bought a green-broke gelding named Bonner, smoothed the rough edges, and decided to let the trail refine old Bonner. Imagine the risk in that. Imagine Charles Horchem, Marion and myself (three guys who had to be entrepreneurs because we don't like to be told what to do) planning the logistics of such a trip. Five horses, two mules, a covered wagon, three trailers and pickups, and all the supplies and food (animal and human) needed for 325 miles on the trail.

A horse or mule accident was almost a certainty. What about arguments among three bull-headed men who were used to being boss? Marion was undeterred. And he was right. His determination and enthusiasm were catching. He had a dream and Charles and I are fortunate that he did. The trip changed our lives in too many ways to describe.

I know that Marion was misunderstood by many, because I share some of his less endearing traits. But misunderstood is probably the wrong word. Marion would say, "I was not misunderstood. I meant exactly what I said. I am what you see and refuse to pretend to be something I'm not." He said what he meant and meant what he said.

And about his tendency to be blunt: I read somewhere that the loss of candor in America is tragic, may yet prove to be mortal, because if we cannot discuss our problems in plain speech that describes reality, it is unlikely we will ever be able to solve those problems. We need more men like Marion, not fewer.

He had integrity and integrity means you are responsible for your life and that you don't blame your problems on others. To borrow Theodore Roosevelt's words, Marion was not "with those cold and timid souls who know neither victory nor defeat."

I have written about our adventures together in *Biscuits Across the Brazos* and incorporated others into my novels. I told many more in *A River of Stories*. I am so sad that he never got to read most of those true tales and got to see none of them in a printed book. He did love books. But I am also very pleased they are there for his family and mine to read. After his death, I wrote about one of our earlier adventures. I hope you enjoy seeing it on the printed pages of a book. And I trust that his children and grandchildren and my own will enjoy it for years to come. What could be better than that?

It Goes Without Sayin'

Writing Marion's eulogy and the previous stories helped heal the sense of loss, but they also brought up a few questions that I can't properly answer. Did I tell him how much he meant to me before he died? If not, why not?

Well, yes and no. I did try to convey my feelings, but my efforts now seem tentative and awkward, certainly not articulate. When I first learned he was ill, I assumed he would recover. There had been previous problems, and he always came through. Marion was tough. We talked about end of life issues, but I tried to keep it light and hopeful, not wishing to examine or even admit the possibility of death. My excuse was that I wanted to keep his spirits up. Close to the end, I did awkwardly tell him how much he meant to me as a cousin, brother, and friend.

But why did we not share our deepest feelings before the specter of illness appeared? Answer—we were raised alike and we weren't raised that way. I don't think he would apologize if the situation were reversed, nor would he want me to. We kept our feelings for each other in our hearts and minds and knew instinctively those feelings grew stronger each year. Letting them out might stop that growth.

Like our fathers before us, we believed that praise owes its value to its scarcity. We also practiced show, not tell. I knew what I meant to him and he knew how much he meant to me. We knew it because we showed it. And somehow, in ways I cannot explain, we feared that telling it would somehow dilute it; take the shine off, so to speak. If we tried to express it, it might not come out right.

Both of us would declare if asked about our feelings for each other, "It goes without sayin.'" My father never told me he loved me until he was on his deathbed, but I never doubted it for a second. I don't necessarily recommend that and I don't follow it with my own children and grandchildren, but that was the way it was back then—and it worked.

Marion had serious trouble with one of his eyes a few years back. On a four- or five-hour round trip to see an ophthalmologist, Marion wanted to talk about his role as a husband, father, grandfather, cousin, brother, uncle and friend. He served as the prosecutor against himself, and I served as defense counsel. I won. Our discussion was serious, and by this strange method, I was able to show him how much I admired his role in each of those capacities without seeming to gush or be overgenerous with praise. I felt better after that trip, and he did, too. How do I know? Because he told someone else who relayed the information to me.

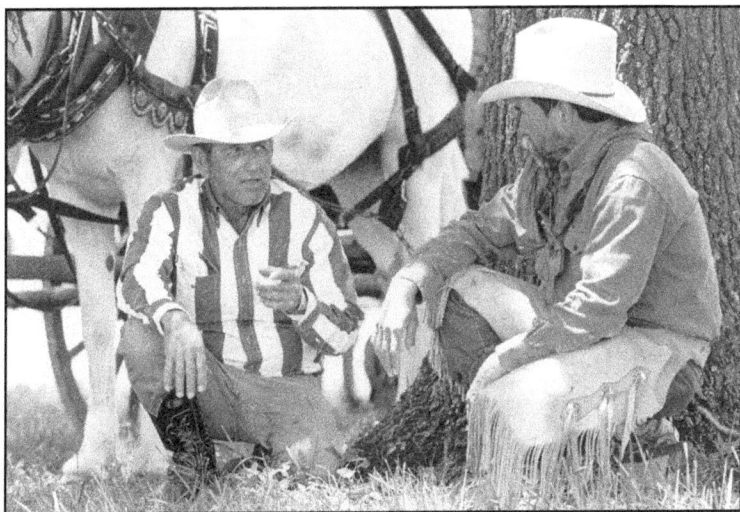

*Since we have gifts that differ according
to the grace given to us, each of us is
to exercise them accordingly.*
—Matthew 12:6

Index